Sulcatas, African Spurred Tortoises in Captivity

(With Notes on Other Popular T...)

by Russ Gurley

Professional Breeders Series™

E C O

© 2005 by ECO Herpetological Publishing & Distribution

ISBN 978-0-9767334-2-0

Copies available from:

ECO Herpetological Publishing & Distribution
915 Seymour Ave. Lansing, MI 48906 USA
telephone: 517.487.5595   fax: 517.371.2709
email: ecoorders@hotmail.com website: http://www.reptileshirts.com

T-Rex Products, Inc.
http://www.t-rexproducts.com

Zoo Book Sales
http://www.zoobooksales.com

LIVING ART publishing
http://www.livingartpublishing.com

Design and layout by Russ Gurley.
Cover design by Rafael Porrata.

Printed in China.

Front Cover: The African Spurred Tortoise, *G. sulcata*. Photo by Russ Gurley.
Back Cover: *G. pardalis*, the Leopard Tortoise. Photo by Bob Ashley.

For Fionnuala and Cait

It is exciting for me when a project becomes complex and convoluted and a variety of friends and colleagues become involved. Several good friends have helped me during the completion of this updated version of my book.

I would like to thank Linda Putnam, Tulsa Zoo, Mark and Kim Bell of Reptile Industries, Jeff and Kim Gee of the Captive Bred Wildlife Foundation, Jeff and Cheryl McIntyre of The Funny Farm, Greg and Leann Christenson, Drew Rheinhardt, Jerry Fife, Binh Pham, Richard Fife, and Rusty Mills for access to tortoises and for their eagerness to help with this project. Photos of their animals and facilities have helped me present the best care and breeding programs in the country.

My friend Bill Love provided some beautiful and creative photos for which he is so widely known. His professionalism and promptness was refreshing. Jim Pether of Reptilandia in the Canary Islands came through with some great photos of *G. sulcata* native habitat and provided some observations of these tortoises in the wild. Sadly, in many areas the African Spurred Tortoises have disappeared or are disappearing.

I would also like to thank Bob and Sheri Ashley of ECO and Eric Thiss of Zoo Book Sales. Without their enthusiasm and prodding, this book would probably not exist.

TABLE OF CONTENTS

INTRODUCTION

The Turtle and Tortoise Preservation Group was established in 1995 to help promote both the protection of wild chelonians and the production of the world's captive chelonians. With the help of some of the best keepers and breeders in the United States, we have been able to establish a captive group of turtles and tortoises that we are proud to manage. During the early days of the TTPG, *Geochelone sulcata*, the African Spurred Tortoise, was being imported in relatively large numbers and we were fortunate enough to work with these great animals. *The African Spurred Tortoise Geochelone sulcata in Captivity* (2003) was the presentation of our early work in written form.

When I was approached to update this book, I was overwhelmed (and proud) to hear that it had sold out of its large print run so quickly. I knew that the numbers of sulcatas being produced probably far exceeded what we had guessed. Now, two years later, these numbers are staggering. Baby African Spurred Tortoises are available in increasing numbers at pet stores, reptile shows, and expos. Unfortunately, many sellers don't have time to spend with the buyer, and they desire to quickly move on to the next sale. Also, many people who sell these little tortoises don't know precisely how to care for them, offering a general over-view of what they know about the care of any baby tortoise.

We believe that there is an often overlooked moral responsibility when learning about captive reptiles to expand not only one's knowledge and skills but also to create an enhanced life for one's animals. I have seen some collections of captive animals that are still kept in antiquated, "ease of maintenance" conditions. These animals sit daily in their tubs or cramped cages, waiting for a mouse, or a hunk of lettuce, living in shadow in a sweater box rack. In other cases, some keepers inspire us with large enclo-sures planted with orchids and bromeliads and sporting high-tech misting systems. Imagine a tortoise living its life in a large vivarium full of cork bark, palm fronds, live plants, clean water, and stimulation. Setting up the enclosure can be quite enjoyable. The search for plants that are native to an animal's habitat and finding the right sand and the special rock can be exciting. Designing and building an environment that stimulates and inspires both the viewer and the animals within can become a mission. We have a choice.

Captive tortoises are worthy of this type of fervor. After all, these ancient creatures are attached to their environment deeply. They have a focus in their eyes and they are led by a finely tuned sense of smell. They search their habitat, dipping their noses into the soil, rubbing their bodies against objects and exploring the other inhabitants of their environment.

The African Spurred Tortoise is at something of a crossroads in captivity these days. As a species, it is catching grief from a variety of fronts. Unfortunately, the reputation of sulcatas is even being damaged by reptile enthusiasts who have self-righteously taken it upon themselves to impose their ideas and lack of understanding onto keepers desiring to work responsibly with these large reptiles.

Sulcata tortoises can inspire individual keepers and entire families. By keeping them properly, children and adults learn respect for a living animal and its needs. Daily routines spring up around this new and exotic pet that instill thoughtfulness and responsibility. With the proliferation of forums and chat rooms on the internet, there has also been a proliferation of care information that is shared, often as gospel. Unfortunately, following some of this information may not be appropriate for many captive situations for sulcata tortoises. There are keepers offering conflicting information and care sheets exist that are not only inconsistent, but even detrimental to the livelihood of these wonderful tortoises.

From a small tan hatchling with wide, alert eyes and a ravenous appetite, these wonderful tortoises quickly (in tortoise terms) can become backyard giants. They grow very large and incredibly heavy with needs that outweigh many keepers' expectations and abilities.

We hope that you find this book helpful whether you are caring for a single hatchling *G. sulcata* or managing a large group of lawn-mowing giants.

Russ Gurley

Director
Turtle and Tortoise Preservation Group
http://www.ttpg.org

Chapter ONE: The African Spurred Tortoise in Nature

Former *G. sulcata* habitat between Dakar and Saint-Louis, Senegal. Sadly, African Spurred Tortoises are no longer found here due to human interference, habitat destruction, and loss of food from the introduction of goats. Photo by Jim Pether.

The African Spurred Tortoise, *Geochelone sulcata,* is the world's third largest tortoise, only smaller than the giant island-dwelling Galapagos and Aldabra tortoises. In nature, this tortoise is found living in a large swath across North-Central Africa south of the Sahara Desert from Mauritania to Ethiopia.

This area of Africa is hot and dry. Temperatures range from the 60s F in the coldest part of winter (June to August in this part of the world) to well over 100° F (38° C) during the summer. Incredibly, this area receives very little rainfall with some areas receiving no rain for several years at a time (Kaplan, 1996).

African Spurred Tortoises are diggers. In fact, they are one of only a few tortoises that burrow extensively in nature. As adults, these giants dig deep tunnels in which to spend the long dry season and to escape the intense heat of the African sun. In addition to some protection from heat and predators, the burrows provide a humid area for absorption of small amounts of moisture as the hot days are exchanged for cooler nights. It is reported that in many areas African Spurred Tortoises are active at dusk and dawn feeding before the heat

The distribution of The African Spurred Tortoise, *Geochelone sulcata*, in nature.

hits (Ernst and Barbour, 1989). Captive observations at the Turtle and Tortoise Preservation Group show this behavior to be not uncommon. In hot dry climates, such as Arizona and southern California, sulcatas are usually active early in the morning and late in the day, spending most of the rest of their day resting in the shade of a shelter or in their burrows.

African Spurred Tortoises feed on grasses, shrubs, and succulent plants in their natural habitat. Most of the moisture they need is obtained from these plants. Their growth in nature is slow and it may take up to 24 years for African Spurred Tortoises to reach maturity in the wild (Lambert, 1993). This is due largely to their life in an environment that is hospitable for only about four months of the year and with eight months of extreme heat and aridity and little vegetation available.

G. sulcata is struggling in the wild. As the people of Africa toil to acquire food, their goats and other livestock are herded into prime feeding habitat. This puts them in direct competition with tortoises for food. African Spurred Tortoises are disappearing,

In nature, *G. sulcata* lives in deep burrows. These burrows allow them to escape the extreme heat of the hottest days. Photo by Jim Pether.

especially in Mali, Chad, Niger, and Ethiopia. In Senegal there are still limited populations in the north and north-east, but overgrazing by cattle is threatening these populations as well (Harrold, 2001).

Chapter TWO: ANATOMY

Massive scaly legs and a muscular head and neck are trademarks of the African Spurred Tortoise. Photo by Bob Ashley.

Evolving in their harsh natural environment has produced in sulcatas an animal that is strong, resilient, and adaptable. Adult African Spurred Tortoises are extremely powerful and heavy with broad, flattened carapaces. They have dry, thick, scaly skin that helps to prevent water loss in their arid homes. These tortoises have the sturdy, broad elephantine feet typical of land tortoises. Both males and females have spurs on the back legs on each side of the tail. These spurs give this species its common name. Males of this awesome tortoise grow up to 30" and commonly reach weights of over 100 pounds. The largest *G. sulcata* recorded was a very large male that was 42" and weighed over 225 pounds (Flower, 1928). Females are typically smaller, reaching only 20 to 24" and weighing from 65 to 75 pounds.

The Shell

Sulcatas are solidly built with a thick, strong shell. They range in color from sandy tan to dark brown in color. The carapace is

Flared marginals and strong curving gulars are seen at the front end of this large male sulcata. Photo by Russ Gurley.

flattened, with grooved seams (sulcata means grooved), and unlike other tortoises, they are nearly square when viewed from above. The plastron features gular projections that are forked. These large, solid gulars are elongated in the males and are used by them for slamming into other male sulcatas and for pushing against other tortoises and obstacles in captivity.

Occasionally, large sulcatas will have a hole in the back marginal scutes. This hole was used for tethering wild-caught specimens to a tree or stake before they were sold and exported.

The Head

The sulcata's head is large and solid. Its eyes are inquisitive, with an unyielding focus, especially if food is nearby. The nasal openings of a healthy African Spurred Tortoise are clear and dry, symbolic of its desert-dwelling life. Its strong jaws are notched above for chopping through coarse vegetable matter and its tongue is large, fleshy, and pink.

The Legs

African Spurred Tortoises have powerful, muscular legs covered with dry, scaly skin. These scales are oversized and thickened, including the two or three large spurs that give this tortoise its common name.

The Tail

Sulcata tails are relatively short in both sexes, but an adult female's tail is significantly shorter than that of the male.

The spurs from which the African Spurred Tortoise gets its name can be seen on the inside of the leg of this large male. Photo by Bob Ashley.

ABNORMALITIES

Pyramiding

Pyramiding is a condition where a tortoise shows abnormal growth on its carapace, making it look bumpy. This is caused when a tortoise eats a diet that is too high in protein and low in calcium. Though most sulcatas that are fed well in captivity show some pyramiding, it is most often seen in captive sulcatas when they are fed solely on commercial foods or when cat food or dog food is added to their diet.

Irregular Scutes

Occasionally, young sulcatas are seen with irregular scutes. This condition occurs in nature, but in captive-hatched specimens these irregular scutes are typically caused when an egg has been incubated on the hot side either accidentally or by a breeder trying to rush the incubation process. These irregular scutes can range from a single small split scute to a spiderweb

Irregular or "split" scutes are somewhat common and do not seem to affect the health of the tortoise. Photo by Bob Ashley.

pattern across the entire back of the carapace.

Soft Shell

Soft shell is a severe malady in tortoises that arises from lack of direct sunlight, lack of dietary calcium, or excessive phosphorus in the diet. Soft shell develops when a tortoise's blood stream shaves calcium from its bones and its shell to meet the calcium needs of the muscular and other body systems, leaving the tortoise's shell soft and pliable. This condition can be corrected by the addition of calcium and vitamin supplements onto the afflicted tortoise's food and by the addition of plenty of natural sunlight which allows the tortoise's body to use this calcium properly.

Chapter THREE: CHOOSING A TORTOISE

A young sulcata should be heavy and alert, and should push against your fingers with force as you hold it in your hand. Photo by Russ Gurley.

If you are thinking about getting an African Spurred Tortoise, there are several things to consider . . .

Spurred Tortoises get very large and require a lot of space and they should be kept outside as much as possible.

Spurred Tortoises need to be kept hot and dry. If they get too damp and cold, they can develop serious medical problems that will probably require a veterinarian's care.

These tortoises do not hibernate so they must be housed indoors or in a warm building during the winter in a temperate environment.

Spurred Tortoises are very strong and spend a great deal of their time digging and pushing against objects. The can do damage to fences, landscaping, and other property.

Spurred Tortoises typically do not mix well with dogs and other tortoises. As male African Spurred Tortoises approach breeding size they may become aggressive, ramming other tortoises, pets, and even people. Recently, at a well-known tortoise breeder's facilities, a large male sulcata rammed, intimidated, and killed a Galapagos Tortoise that was nearly twice its height and weight.

Well cared for African Spurred Tortoises can live for many years, so they will require a long-term obligation.

If you weigh all of these considerations and are willing to make the commitment, then a Spurred Tortoise may be right for you.

FINDING A TORTOISE

Once you decide to get a sulcata tortoise and after you have read as much as you can find about these tortoises, the search begins.

Pet and Specialty Stores

As interest grows, more and more pet stores are offering tortoises for sale. Not only are they offering tortoises for pets, but they are exhibiting healthy animals in proper and inspiring set-ups. Many are offering correct advice and stocking the best equipment and supplies for their customers. In the past, pet stores rarely established proper enclosures to keep tortoises long-term. Heating and diet were inappropriate and specimens were often in poor health and species from all over the world were mixed together in a single, large cage. As imported specimens made up most of the tortoises for sale in the shops, most were traumatized and parasitized. Now, with the increased emphasis on the true needs of tortoises, shops are installing larger enclosures with basking spots and they are offering a healthy diet. Many are even offering veterinary services to care for tortoises before or during sales times.

Though many continue to get a bad rap, these shops are literally the front line in the crusade to educate the general public about tortoises. As the first stop for most people searching for a pet tortoise, pet stores have the unique ability to inspire a beginning tortoise keeper's first creative ideas and to offer proper procedures for setting up and caring for animals.

Choosing a Specific Tortoise

When you discover a tortoise that you are interested in purchasing, begin by checking out the tortoise's enclosure. Check the substrate. It should be clean and tortoises should not be crowded. If tortoises from different parts of the world are kept together, especially in crowded conditions, we suggest you don't buy any.

Ask about the tortoise that has caught your eye. Was it bred by the person you are talking to? Was it bred locally? What's it been through over the last few days? Was it purchased from a breeder? Was it purchased from a dealer? Was it shipped? If the salesperson gets irritated, assure them that you are not trying to track down their sources and that you are just trying to see what this tortoise has been through prior to your purchase.

Pick up the tortoise. It should be alert, active, and heavy.

Check its strength. It should push off of your fingers with force.

Check its uniformity. The shape of the scutes should not be irregular and there should be no noticeable bumps, lumps, or asymmetry to its body. The profile should also be symmetrical.

Check its eyes. They should not be puffy and should be clear, mucus-free, and alert.

Check its nostrils. The nostrils should be open and free from any bubbles or discharge.

Check its mouth. The mouth should be free from injuries, irregularities, or lumps.

Babies should be chosen from a clean, warm enclosure with food and shelter. These will be from a breeder that has obviously cared for them properly. Photo by Russ Gurley.

Check its vent. Its cloacal opening and tail should be free of any discharge or lumps.

Ask about any guarantee the seller might offer. Is this guarantee offered in writing? Remember, your choice is often final and you will have no possibility of a refund. In fairness, the seller can't know your facilities or the care you will offer and so can only guarantee the tortoise's current health.

Shows and Expos

In recent years, reptile shows and expos have become very popular. In the last few years there has been an increase in the number of captive-produced turtles and tortoises at these shows. Typically, the specimens offered at these shows are healthy, feeding well, and excellent specimens to begin a tortoise-keeping hobby or to add to an existing collection. At these shows you get the rare opportunity to hand pick the animal you want to purchase. When having a tortoise shipped to you, there is always the risk of receiving a tortoise that is picked by someone who

The most successful tortoise breeders typically offer their tortoises large sunny outdoor enclosures to enhance natural behaviors. Courtesy of the Captive Bred Wildlife Foundation. Photo by Bob Ashley.

may not have your best interest at heart. Add to the savings of not having to pay shipping and the lack of stress placed on the animal from shipping and the shows and expos are often an excellent opportunity to get a really nice tortoise.

The top U.S. shows include the National Reptile Breeders Expo in Florida and the N.A.R.B.C. shows in Anaheim, Chicago, and Philadelphia. There are dozens of other great local shows throughout the country. These shows can be located on the internet, through local herpetological societies, and they are advertised in reptile magazines and journals. It is well worth the effort to track them down.

Tortoise Breeders

Some keepers are fortunate to have a local tortoise breeder near their home. Often these breeders will welcome visitors (potential customers) to their facilities. In this situation, you get to see the breeder's facilities and see his or her animals. You might learn some of their tricks, glean some experience and helpful hints from them, and often gain a new friend or colleague with which to share ideas and offspring. You can find these breeders through a local herp society, ads in a reptile magazine, or on the internet.

The Internet

The internet has very quickly developed into a source of live animals. There are several extensive websites that offer classified ad sections where you can order animals and plants as well as heat lamps, UV bulbs, cages, vitamins, food, and more. There have been occasional problems with unscrupulous, faceless dealers. You don't get to see the facilities and many of these internet dealers are simply buying and reselling animals. Some don't disclose to beginners that an animal is captive-produced or wild-caught, or even worse lie and say that it is when it isn't. There are also concerns about shipping, even with overnight delivery services. There are Styrofoam-lined boxes, disposable heat packs, and most boxes can travel across the country in a day without a problem. However, we have received boxes from supposedly professional dealers that had a half dozen animals stuffed into a pillowcase and placed into an empty box. No packing material, no Styrofoam liner, and a resulting disastrous event.

If you are careful and inquisitive, these internet dealers can be a good source for tortoises. When contacting people selling tortoises, ask plenty of questions. These people want to sell you a live tortoise (or tortoises) and keep you as a future customer so they should be willing to spend a little extra time with you. Make sure they are charging a fair price by looking around at what these animals typically sell for in other ads and from other sources such as pet stores, breeders, and dealer price lists. Do your homework. Most sellers will be willing to send you photos of the specific animal in which you are interested. Find out about their packing and shipping techniques. Make sure they sound logical and safe for the animal. If the seller is rude or unwilling to answer your questions, move on and count your blessings. Typically, these deals end up being the ones you regret.

There is some confusion about which shipping companies will

ship turtles and tortoises. Currently, it depends on the company, where you live, and how knowledgeable the individual who helps you is. Check around locally with carriers offering overnight service. As an individual, the airline freight companies will not be able to work with you. For "unknown shippers" shipping by air freight is nearly impossible except for the large dealers that have been willing to jump through the required "hoops". Your best bet is the big companies offering overnight shipping such as DHL, Federal Express, and UPS.

United States Postal Service
USPS regulation: United States Postal Service, Hazardous, Restricted, and Perishable Material, Publication 52, 1999 525.3 Reptiles – All snakes, turtles, and poisonous reptiles are nonmailable.

"Turtles are the only living members of the subclass Anapsida, which is characterized by a primitive skull with a solid cranium and no temporal openings (anapsid). These shelled reptiles constitute the order Testudines. All living shelled reptiles are turtles, but the terms tortoise and terrapin have also been applied, and these have different meanings in various parts of the world. Tortoise is best applied to terrestrial turtles. Terrapin is usually applied to edible, more or less aquatic, hard-shelled turtles."

Turtles of the World
C.H. Ernst, R.G.M. Altenburg, and R.W. Barbour

Shipping Tortoises

Place the animal carefully into a pillow case or cloth bag. (Occasionally, we place smaller tortoises into a small cardboard box, similar in size to a shoe box that has been perforated with lots of holes and stuffed full of dry or lightly dampened sphagnum moss.) Place the animals so that they are fairly tightly packed inside. This prevents them from banging their legs around or injuring their head or neck when the box is moved.

Place the bag or small box into a larger, Styrofoam-lined cardboard shipping box. These boxes are available on the internet (http://superiorenterprise.com) or through your local pet store as they are used to transport tropical fish. They usually cost from $8.00 to $10.00 each.)

Fill in around the pillow case or small box with packing material such as biodegradable "peanuts" or wadded up newspaper. Again, make sure that the animals cannot bang around inside the box. They don't need to crawl or stretch out as they travel. If they can breathe easily and not get injured when the box is bounced around, they will be safest.

Styrofoam-lined boxes are excellent for shipping and transporting tortoises. Photo by Kevin McCurley.

Tape the box shut securely with strapping tape.

During hot months, we perforate each side of the outer box and Styrofoam liner with six to eight holes about the diameter of a pencil. Make sure the holes are in the outer cardboard box and the inner Styrofoam liner. During cooler months or when traveling during a cold night, we only add two or three perforations in each side. Most reptile shippers feel that the small openings around the flaps of the box, Styrofoam lid, etc. offer enough air in and out during the relatively short travel time.

Label the box LIVE HARMLESS REPTILES or LIVE TORTOISES and PERISHABLE and note which end is up on the top and sides of the box. (We often add PLEASE AVOID EXTREME HEAT or PLEASE AVOID EXTREME COLD as well.)

Quarantine

Even with a captive-hatched sulcata, we suggest a quarantine period of 30 to 45 days before you add it to your existing collection. Many new keepers will even choose to have a fecal sample checked by a local veterinarian just to be safe.

TTPG Rule: Don't mix species together. We feel that this is very important on many different levels. The requirements of other species of tortoises such as Red-footed Tortoises and Yellow-footed Tortoises are radically different than those of your Spurred Tortoise. Red-footed Tortoises and Yellow-footed Tortoises like it hot and humid. Central Asian (Russian) Tortoises require similar captive conditions to African Spurred Tortoises but are not a good species to mix with African species. Leopard Tortoises like it hot and dry and get quite large. Many keepers mix Spurred Tortoises and Leopard Tortoises. We know of cases where aggressive Spurred Tortoises have rammed and injured Leopard Tortoises. Leopard Tortoises are typically shy and sensitive and will stress out very quickly if shoved and prodded by the incessant attacks of even much smaller sulcatas. In addition, it is felt by most keepers that bacteria, viruses, and parasites can be passed from one tortoise species to another and the results may be more harmful than a simple cross-contamination.

Chapter FOUR: INDOOR ENCLOSURES

This large terrarium provides the ideal indoor home for a small sulcata. Photo by Russ Gurley.

Raising a sulcata tortoise indoors is tricky. Though they have proven to be extremely hardy in a variety of environments, they have a very close relationship with the sun and the heat and UV rays that it provides. If a keeper is diligent, he or she can provide the nutritional supplements and heat that this species requires in an indoor situation. One should however, let these tortoises live outside whenever possible. We have found the best indoor enclosures for African Spurred Tortoises to be glass terrariums, tubs, and stock tanks. Glass terrariums are easy to find at a local pet shop or at a reptile show. They are usually inexpensive, come in a variety of sizes, and are easy to clean and sterilize. A keeper should choose a terrarium that is longer than it is tall so the tortoise can have plenty of room to exercise. Also a secure top is needed when children or other pets have access to the enclosure.

A 20-gallon long terrarium with a shelter, UVB and heat-emitting bulb, shallow water dish, and safe substrate are the requirements for housing a small tortoise. Photo by Russ Gurley.

Small Tortoises

Glass Terrariums

The first enclosure for a small tortoise can be a terrarium in the 10 to 20 gallon range. We have found 20-gallon long aquariums to be ideal. The length of these aquariums (30" l x 12" w x 12" h) gives you a good space to establish a temperature gradient within the enclosure. By placing a clamp type fixture with a 75-watt bulb over one end, the keeper can establish the required 90° to 95° F (32° to 35° C) basking spot that is essential for growing African Spurred Tortoises. The length of the long enclosure typically allows the other end to stay in the 80° to 85° F (27° to 29° C) range. Be careful. Don't put these glass enclosures outside in the sun. Glass aquariums can heat up very quickly and though heat-lovers, these little tortoises can dehydrate and die quickly if they are not given access to some shade via a shelter.

There is no need for a top to this enclosure unless you need it to support heat lamps or light fixtures or if you have small children or pets that will be likely to get into the enclosure.

Substrate

There are almost as many ideas about the proper substrate for small tortoises as there are tortoise keepers. Many breeders suggest using paper towel as it is easy to clean and is inexpensive. When the towel gets soiled, it can be easily removed and replaced with new.

Rabbit pellets are a good substrate because they are made from compressed alfalfa hay. If the small tortoise is a sloppy eater, and gets some chunks of the rabbit pellets as it feeds, they simply add to its meal.

A sand and peat mixture is a natural substrate and supports the naturalistic captive environment ideal that we promote. With the addition of rocks, wood, and plants (protected from the voracious tortoises by rock barriers or large clay pots) one can design an interesting and exciting tortoise enclosure. Some keepers are concerned about young tortoises accidentally ingesting sand as they eat. We feed our tortoises on small trays or plates so there is little access to the substrate while they are eating. Over the years, we have never lost a tortoise to sand impaction.

Heat and Lighting

The hobby of keeping turtles and tortoises has grown dramatically in the last five years. With this growth has been an associated proliferation of products related to their care. Much of the information about these products is misleading or confusing for new keepers. Among the most confusing of these products are the lighting and heating accessories.

Heat

For heat, we suggest a clip lamp fixture and an incandescent bulb in the 75 to 100 watt range. These bulbs provide heat in a "basking spot" area which is important to most tortoise species. As mentioned above, high heat and aridity with a temperature gradient ranging from 80° F (27° C) to 95° F (35° C) is necessary to keep these tortoises healthy. We mount the fixture about 12" above the substrate to provide a hot spot for the tortoises. During the winter or in cooler rooms, we add a reptile heating pad on the low setting underneath the "hot" end of their vivarium for a little added heat.

Lighting and Nutrition

Sun-loving, diurnal species such as the African Spurred Tortoise require Vitamin D3 for the metabolism of calcium in their bodies. They produce this Vitamin D3 by absorbing UV rays from the sun. Vitamin D3 is not found in plant material, so vitamin supplements containing D3 can be added to the diet which will essentially simulate this process. For those species tied closely to the sun, there is no question that the addition of natural sunlight is beneficial, even with the proper use of dietary supplements.

Captive tortoises not exposed to natural sunlight and those not exposed to an artificial source of high-quality UVB emissions run a very real risk of developing metabolic bone disease (MBD). MBD is a dangerous condition that occurs most commonly in young tortoises that are growing quickly and in egg-laying females. This condition leaves tortoises with soft, pliable shells and growth deformities that are not only abnormal, but

Heat can be provided via bulbs in clamp type fixtures above the enclosure. UVB-emitting bulbs can be placed in shoplight fixtures overhead. Photo by Russ Gurley.

also life-threatening. In fact, it is reported that MBD is the most common cause of death in many types of young, captive reptiles (Highfield, 2002).

There are dozens of fluorescent and incandescent bulbs on the market and available through pet stores that bill themselves as "full spectrum", "basking lights", "reptile bulbs", etc. However, there are very few that actually emit the UVB rays needed for the proper utilization of calcium by captive reptiles. A few, including Active UV-heat bulbs® by T-REX, Zoomed's Reptisun 5.0® bulbs have actually proven to effectively boost and restore Vitamin D3 levels in reptilian blood and we have seen increased activity and more "natural" behaviors in our captive reptiles. These bulbs work well as long as a few important conditions are observed.

These bulbs need to be placed from 12" to 18" above the animals. Further distances greatly reduce their efficiency.
The rays emitted from these bulbs must not be obstructed by plastic, plexiglass, or glass. They must be mounted above an open enclosure or must rest on a screen top of some sort.
These bulbs need to be replaced at least once each year. (Active UV-heat bulbs® by T-REX reportedly last considerably longer than the others mentioned.) We mark each bulb with a marker noting the date it was installed so we know when to replace it.

We use shop light fixtures or fluorescent aquarium fixtures with two high-quality UVB bulbs (ZOOMED's Reptisun 5.0® bulbs) and one incandescent fixture with an Active UV-heat bulb® above all of our indoor turtles and tortoises. We feel that this combination of bulbs puts out a sufficient amount of UVB indoors and they are used alongside the added vitamin and calcium supplementation.

In addition to lighting, many reptile keepers are now experiment-ing with controlling the calcium needs of their captives through diet rather than access to sunlight. Some believe that when offered in the proper proportions (Vitamin D3 along with 2 parts calcium to 1 part phosphorus), dietary supplementation can provide the needs of most diurnal reptiles.

A sulcata should be given a shelter in which it can escape the heat of the heat lamp and where it will feel secure. Photo by Russ Gurley.

Shelter / Cage Decorations

Security and an escape from the heat can be offered by a variety of shelters. Large pieces of cork bark, drift wood, commercial shelters, and even upside-down shoe boxes with a doorway, make excellent shelters for small tortoises.

Medium Tortoises

Glass Terrariums

The enclosure for a medium sulcata can be an aquarium in the 40 to 60 gallon range or a medium tub or stock tank. We have found the shorter and longer aquariums to be ideal. Once again, choose a terrarium that gives you enough space to establish a temperature gradient within the enclosure. Ex: 40 gallon breeder - (48"l x 13" w x 16" h) - 58 gallon - (36" l x 18" w x 21" h).

Tubs

A variety of plastic / polyethylene tubs are available to tortoise keepers. We suggest purchasing the largest ones possible for your available space. Watching tortoises from above is an interesting change for most keepers. There is often a feeling of watching them in their world -

Large tubs make ideal homes for medium sulcatas.
Photo by Russ Gurley.

a natural area far from the hustle and bustle of everyday life.

Our medium tubs are 72" l x 36" w x 12" h. Tubs this size are produced by a few different companies and are distributed by specialty pet stores and several herp supply retailers. We have used VISION tubs® and Waterlandtubs®. They are lightweight and easy to move and clean. We have found them both to be excellent enclosures for small and medium tortoises.

Stock Tanks

In most parts of the country, galvanized metal or plastic stock tanks are available in a variety of shapes and sizes from farm and garden stores. We have used these tanks in indoor and outdoor settings for terrestrial, semi-aquatic, and aquatic species with success. The metal ones are thicker-walled, which makes them somewhat heavier than the other tubs, but they have several advantages including depth (24"), strength and sturdiness, a variety of sizes and shapes, and a pre-drilled drain hole. Their oval and round shapes sometimes fit easier into a turtle keeper's established space.

Substrate

A sand and peat mixture is a natural and inexpensive substrate in these larger enclosures. With the addition of rocks, wood, and plants (protected from the voracious tortoises by rock barriers or large clay pots), one can design an interesting and exciting tortoise enclosure. Rabbit pellets are a good substrate for tortoises in these tubs because they are inexpensive .

Heat

As mentioned above, high heat and aridity with a temperature gradient is necessary to keep these tortoises healthy. In the medium-sized enclosures we typically use a clip lamp fixture with an incandescent bulb mounted about 12" above the substrate to provide a hot spot for the tortoises. This hot spot is kept at 90° to 95° F (32° to 35° C). During the winter we add an extra heat lamp or place an inexpensive heating pad underneath the tub for a little added heat.

Lighting

We use shop light fixtures with high-quality UVB bulbs such as ZOOMED's Reptisun 5.0® bulbs and a T-Rex Active UV-heat® bulb above all of our indoor turtles and tortoises.

Shelters

Security and an escape from the heat are offered by a variety of shelters. Cork bark, large pieces of drift wood, and large commercial shelters make excellent safe places for medium-sized tortoises.

Big Tortoises

From the photos and text already encountered here, you will now know that sulcata tortoises get very large. Even though this process takes a relatively long time (5 to 8 years or more in captivity) you must have a plan in place. With some modifications, you will be able to keep your large tortoise well indoors for periods of time. Be aware that if you keep large sulcatas inside, they will require a large tub or stock tank. Many keepers have even used a utility room or a basement. Be aware that these large tortoises will produce a large amount of waste and very soon your house will reek of tortoise feces. Even with diligent daily care the smell will persist. Add to this the fact that indoor sulcatas that roam free will wreck your furniture and terrorize your pets. These are just a couple of reasons why large sulcatas should be outside.

Tubs

If your tortoises are kept for some time indoors, we suggest purchasing the largest tubs possible for your available space.

At the TTPG, our largest tubs are 84" l x 48" w x 24" h. Tubs this size are produced by a few different companies and are distributed by several herp supply retailers. We have used large VISION tubs® and large Waterlandtubs® with success. We have found them to be excellent winter enclosures for several medium tortoises or one large tortoises. These tubs are relatively lightweight and easy to move and clean.

Stock Tanks

In most parts of the country, galvanized metal or plastic stock tanks are available in a variety of sizes and shapes. They are sturdy and somewhat heavier than the other tubs, but they have several advantages including depth (24"), strength and sturdiness, and a variety of sizes and shapes.

Stock tanks can make excellent indoor enclosures for larger tortoises. Photo by Binh Pham.

Substrate

These larger enclosures leave you fewer options for substrate. Cypress mulch, hardwood mulch, and a sand and peat mixture are all natural substrates that work well for larger sulcatas. Rabbit pellets are good because they are inexpensive and easy to clean and/or replace.

Heat

We use a clip lamp fixture mounted above the substrate to provide a hot spot of 95° F (35° C) for even the largest tortoises. Indoors, during the winter, we add a second or third lamp and occasionally a large reptile heating pad under their enclosure for a little extra heat.

In areas with cold winters, keepers will often add a gas or electric heater. Be sure to keep this heater raised off the floor or have it mounted securely so tortoises can't tip it over and start a fire. Heat lamps can be added for extra heat as well. These lamps can be placed on timers for the addition of daytime heat.

Fiberglass furrowing pads ("pig blankets") can also be added for extra heat from beneath.

Lighting

We use shop light fixtures with high-quality UVB bulbs and one T-Rex Active UV-heat® bulb in a clip fixture above our indoor tortoise enclosures.

Shelter / Cage Decorations

Larger tortoises are very destructive when it comes to cage decorations. We have found that adding a few piles of prairie hay or straw into these enclosures gives them a place to feel secure. They often sleep under these piles of hay.

Most sulcata keepers establish indoor winter quarters for large tortoises. These winter quarters can be inside a home or in an outbuilding or greenhouse. These buildings are usually divided into stalls or large stock tanks are set up inside for separating males and for separating smaller and larger specimens.

Chapter FIVE: OUTDOOR ENCLOSURES

Outdoor enclosures should provide plenty of plants, shelter, fresh water, and areas for exercise. Courtesy of Linda Putnam. Photo by Russ Gurley.

The benefits of natural sunlight and outdoor heat for a sun-loving tortoise from arid Africa are obvious. Also, the large size attained by *G. sulcata* makes it a prime candidate for outdoor enclosures.

Small Tortoises

Even small (2-6") African Spurred Tortoises should be offered outdoor enclosures. They can be kept quite easily in tubs and tanks or in pens fashioned from posts or railroad ties. Smaller enclosures can be used, but always offer your tortoises as much space as possible, especially outdoors. The substrate can be sand or a sand-peat mixture or a pesticide- and herbicide-free patch of lawn. Add some nice pieces of cork bark, driftwood, and plenty of vegetation such as ornamental grasses and piles of leaves to add a feeling of security and to offer the little tortoises

In many areas, outdoor enclosures will need a strong, secure lid to dissuade predators. Courtesy of Kurt Edwards. Photo by Russ Gurley.

some shade. You can also add some shade over the top of part of their enclosure with a nearby tree or "roof" made of a wooden plank or piece of shade cloth.

In some areas, it is imperative that the top of the enclosure is securely covered to keep out predators. We have used tops made from a wooden frame with strong hardware cloth attached. This secure top will keep predators out and let UV rays through. Don't use window screening, as it will typically not deter predators. Predators of smaller tortoises can include raccoons, opossums, large birds, dogs and cats, foxes, coyotes, and even ants in some areas.

Nowadays many keepers have to add locks to their outdoor tortoise enclosures. Theft by humans is becoming more and more common as people discover the value of these tortoises or are attracted by their awesome size.

Even sun-loving species will need some shelter to feel secure and to escape the heat. Courtesy of Drew Rheinhardt. Photo by Russ Gurley.

Medium Tortoises

Outdoors, medium-sized (8-12") sulcatas can live in similar, only larger pens or enclosures.

Sulcatas do very well in a pen on the ground. We stack railroad ties or landscape posts into a variety of sizes and shapes. You will need to drive metal or wooden stakes to reinforce the pen, even for medium tortoises. They are so strong! Add a shelter or two inside. These shelters can be small doghouses, homemade structures, or clumps of ornamental grasses. Shrubs, succulent plants, cacti, and small trees will add to the beauty of any outdoor sulcata enclosure. These plants must be protected by being placed up on rocks or concrete blocks. If it is in reach of the tortoises, it will no doubt be eaten very quickly.

Large Tortoises

Large African Spurred Tortoises will require big, secure outdoor enclosures or an entire back yard in which to roam. A sturdy fence is a must and will probably need to be reinforced with concrete blocks or staked railroad ties as large sulcatas tend to "test" fences by pushing and digging.

If their enclosure is fenced, a stockade or privacy fence is much better than a chain link fence because without a visual barrier the tortoise will usually spend a great deal of time trying to push through to get to "greener pastures" on the other side. An insistent tortoise can injure itself by pushing against the chain link and scrapes to its legs and face and even eye injuries are possible. If its vision is blocked by a visual barrier, the tortoise will usually focus on the environment at hand.

Though they love it hot and dry, sulcatas do need some shade and hiding places for resting in the hottest parts of the day. This can be accomplished using shrubs and plants or with manmade structures such as doghouses. Keepers in some areas will be able to get creative and plant fruit trees such as apple, pear, peach, mango, fig, and large *Opuntia* cactus plants for shade. These trees will not only provide shade, but also will provide tasty treats as the fruit ripens and falls.

Interestingly, captive sulcatas love a water hole to soak in during the heat of summer. You should try to never have standing water in a sulcata pen for any length of time because it can harbor

Large tortoises can do damage to most wooden fences and pens so keepers often use rock and concrete structures to house their largest and most powerful specimens. Courtesy of The Funny Farm. Photo by Russ Gurley.

If given the opportunity, sulcatas will spend a great deal of time soaking in fresh water. Photo by Bob Ashley.

harmful bacteria and it can be a breeding ground for mosquitoes. Also, sulcata skin is very permeable to water and absorbing large amounts of water is unnatural for them. We suggest letting them soak only once a week during summer and once every 2-3 weeks during the cooler months.

During the hottest days, sulcatas will spend time resting in shallow water or in mud baths. Photo by Russ Gurley.

African Spurred Tortoises can dig large and deep burrows in an outdoor enclosure. These are typically dug when tortoises need a secure shelter but may simply be a part of their daily activities. Photo by Bob Ashley.

The sulcata Burrow

As mentioned, it is natural behavior for a sulcata tortoise to dig. In the wild, they dig deep burrows. These burrows provide shelter, protection, and some humidity. In captivity, some sulcatas will be enthusiastic diggers and others will not dig, tending to crawl under existing shelters instead. If your sulcata has access to water, shade, and plenty of secure hiding spaces, they will probably not dig. However, some individuals will be diggers and they will be difficult to dissuade. The problem with digging, other than wrecking your yard, is that sulcatas with burrows can occasionally crawl deep into their long burrow on a cold night. If they are not retrievable, they could get chilled, which can lead to respiratory problems, pneumonia, and even death.

Winter Quarters

In moderately warm areas (winters down to 45° F), keepers and breeders typically add doghouses modified to hold heat into their outdoor sulcata pens. A fixture with an incandescent bulb is placed inside or a "pig blanket" is placed underneath the doghouse to add warmth on cold nights. The goal is to keep the tortoises in the 60° to 65° F range. Tortoises will typically come out during the sunny days, even when it is cool (50° to 55° F), and retreat to the warmth of their shelter in the early evening. In this situation, keepers

A large sulcata walks up the ramp and into the warmth of its winter shelter. Photo by Russ Gurley.

must check on their tortoises during cold nights to make sure they get inside okay.

In regions with cold winters (below 45° F), your sulcatas will need to be brought indoors to prevent cold-related problems such as respiratory infections and pneumonia. Many keepers choose to keep stock tanks inside in a special warm room and carry their tortoises inside each evening. The large scale tortoise keepers usually have insulated buildings or greenhouses constructed to keep their tortoises warm during winter. These buildings or greenhouses can be purchased in kit form from local home improvement centers. Also, the classified ads in the newspaper are a good source for a small building. Look under "Portable Buildings". They can usually be purchased and moved relatively inexpensively.

Stalls or divisions can be added within these buildings to keep the males and females or aggressive individuals separated. Though fighting behavior is usually low during the cool winter, tortoises

Inside the winter quarters there is a deep bedding of cypress mulch and hay and heat lamps to keep the area warm. Photo by Russ Gurley.

will occasionally still ram each other and possibly injure one another.

Sulcatas are intelligent and will usually instinctively move into and out of their cool weather buildings. They emerge during a sunny day to feed and when a cold evening arrives, they will usually be where they are supposed to be. If they get under a shrub or tree roots, under a building, or in a burrow when a cold night hits, they can get a chill and leave you battling a respiratory infection all winter. This is a common occurrence in tortoise collections in northern parts of the United States, Canada, and much of Europe. If you find that you need to move a big tortoise inside during cold weather, it can be problematic. You have a couple of choices: First, you may have to carry it. This can be difficult, even for two people, once you have a large specimen weighing 75 to 100 pounds or more. Secondly, you might be able to lure a large *G. sulcata* with its favorite food such as an aromatic fruit like banana or melon or a brightly colored one such as an apple or tomato. (This is not easy when they are cold and sluggish!)

HELPFUL HINTS

CAUTION: Be sure to "baby-proof" your outdoor enclosure. First, look for any items that might cause your tortoise to tumble over onto its back. Tortoises can turn over and if unable to right themselves, they can die very quickly, especially on a hot day. The weight of their internal organs pressing down on their lungs (now on the bottom) can also be a fatal situation. This is an occurrence that is very dangerous and many captive tortoises are lost to this type of accident. Objects that can cause a tortoise to accidentally flip over include stairs, low enclosure walls, concrete blocks, and even each other. Also, males will occasionally flip each other over when pushing each other around the yard.

Shell damage from ramming can occur in these powerful tortoises. These injuries and the related stress can be fatal. However, once a hierarchy is established, these bouts usually occur only during breeding season. Subordinate males and smaller tortoises are smart and usually know when to avoid larger males and choose to beat a hasty retreat when one wanders near.

Make sure that a tortoise cannot come into contact with pesticides and herbicides through their food or captive environment.

Sulcatas and other tortoises are attracted to colorful fruit and flowers and therefore also to small colorful objects like plastic toys and even plastic bags. They will eat these objects and if not passed in the feces, they can cause veterinary emergencies.

Sulcatas are ravenous feeders on just about any plant material. Unlike most tortoises, they use the "eat first and ask questions later" feeding method. They will even eat poisonous plants or plant parts if given the opportunity. Signs of poisoning include lethargy, droopy head, drooling, and bloody or loose stools. Check your tortoise area and consult the list in the chapter on Health for the most common poisonous plants found in yards.

Who Will Be Man's Best Friend?

Dogs and tortoises do not mix! Although many tortoise keepers keep both as pets, it is really unwise to mix dogs and tortoises. The pattern is quite typical. . . Even after living with them peacefully for a while, curiosity and innate behavior gets the best of the dog and soon you will have problems. Dogs will chew on large tortoises, will kill little ones, and will produce feces that the tortoises will eat. For some reason, sulcatas love to eat dog feces. Many African tortoises will seek out hyena feces in the wild as a source of calcium (the ground up bones in the waste). Perhaps this is what is happening with sulcatas? In any event, it is unnatural and a possible source for parasitic infection for your tortoises. As most dog owners know, dogs commonly harbor at least one or two types of parasitic worms. These worms, when transmitted to an exotic species such as your tortoise, might cause more harm than a typical mild worm infection. At the least, these parasites rob your tortoises of nutrition, strength, energy, and livelihood.

Chapter SIX: FEEDING

A group of large, breeder African Spurred Tortoises enjoying a meal of tomatoes and red bell peppers. Photo by Rusty Mills.

African Spurred Tortoises eat a lot! They are browsers who actively munch leaves and trim grass of its nutritious tips. In the wild their diet is high in fiber, low in protein, and very low in fat. This low nutrition diet leads to slow growth and a daily routine spent searching for food and moisture in a very harsh environment.

Unlike this life in nature, captive African Spurred Tortoises are presented with an abundance of food and a veritable smorgasbord by thoughtful keepers. Usually, new owners experiment with a variety of food and both natural and commercial diets are considered. Care must be taken, however, to make sure that tortoises receive a diet that recreates their natural intake of food as closely as possible. For sulcata keepers, the goal is to provide a diet that has lots of fiber, but is low in protein and fat content.

The ideal foods for your African Spurred Tortoise are grasses, prairie hay, clover, dandelions, and a variety of leaves. They also

Large sulcatas will eat an incredible amount of groceries each week. It is a good idea to establish a relationship with your local produce growers for their old vegetables. Photo by Russ Gurley.

enjoy dark green lettuce, kale, carrot tops, broccoli, squash, and more. In addition to these, your tortoise can feed on flowers (see Poisonous Plant list), alfalfa hay (modest amounts as it is high in protein and calcium), and a variety of other plant material. Spineless *Opuntia* cactus pads are a very good food for all tortoises (Check the vegetable section of your local grocery that offers a variety of Hispanic foods).

Great Supplemental Foods for your Sulcata Tortoise:

> Romaine lettuce
> Red leaf lettuce
> Green leaf lettuce
> Collard greens
> Kale
> Carrot tops and carrots
> Squash
> Red cabbage

Sweet potatoes
Pumpkin
Melons *
Cantaloupe *
Banana *
Apples (no seeds) *
Pears (no seeds) *
Clover
Geraniums
Hibiscus
Nasturtium
Rose

* Feed fruit to *G. sulcata* only sparingly because of the high sugar content.

We add a sprinkle of multivitamin powder and calcium with Vitamin D3 onto our tortoises' salads every 5-6 feedings. For growing babies and reproductive females, we add the calcium-vitamin mixture every 2-3 feedings.

Nutritional Analysis of Some Commercially Available Diets

MAZURI Tortoise Diet®
Protein – not less than 15.0%
Fat – not less than 3.0%
Fiber – not more than 18.0%

ZOOMED Box Turtle and Land Tortoise Food®
Protein – max. 18.4%
Fat – min. 5.2%
Fiber – max. 10.0%

Flukers Tortoise Diet®
Protein – not less than 15.0%
Fat – not less than 3.0%
Fiber – not more than 18.0%

Pretty Pets Tortoise Food®
Protein – 8.0%
Fat – 3.0%
Fiber – 13.0%

Rep-Cal Tortoise Food®
Protein – 19.0%
Fat – 1.0%
Fiber – 18.0%

Most of these commercial foods are more suited to Red-footed Tortoises, Yellow-footed Tortoises, and Hinge-backed Tortoises as these species normally take in larger amounts of protein through eating carrion and invertebrates in the wild.

Water

It should be abundantly obvious by now that African Spurred Tortoises love it hot and dry. Their natural habitat, with its arid, sandy soil with few shrubs and dry grasses, sees very little water. Interestingly, in captivity these tortoises seem to be attracted to water and will spend a lot of time soaking in pools of rainwater or areas where a garden hose has been left running.

It is a good idea to limit the amount of soaking they do and we feel that it is never a good idea to leave pools of standing water in an outdoor sulcata enclosure. These pools can be breeding grounds for bacteria and mosquitoes. Instead, find a very large flat dish like those used under flower pots. Keep fresh water available for them in these dishes. They are also easy to clean and sterilize. We clean them once a week (or when needed) with a light bleach solution and let them air dry in the sun when possible.

When they are small, soak young tortoises in a flat dish of purified room temperature water. We suggest soaking babies and juveniles once a week, especially in the summer and we offer the large tortoises additional water once every ten days to two weeks during the hottest part of the year. Be careful that the water

Young sulcatas should be taken from their enclosure and soaked in shallow, tepid water once a week. Photo by Bob Ashley.

level is only up to a point just above the edge of the plastron (covering the legs). We suggest soaking them once a week. Soak them for just a few minutes while you clean the cage or remove feces or leftover greens from their enclosure.

Chapter SEVEN: HEALTH

African Spurred Tortoises are occasionally encountered with shell anomalies resulting from injuries from fighting or from incubation problems. Photo by Bob Ashley.

Captive African Spurred Tortoises are very hardy and tolerant of a wide range of captive conditions. However, occasional accidents or lapses in good husbandry produce a tortoise with an ailment or injury. Watch for respiratory distress, weight loss, runny stools, and physical changes. These are all signs of a problem.

If a tortoise is alert and feeding, it is fairly easy for a keeper to treat minor problems. If a tortoise is lethargic and refusing to eat or is suffering from a more serious problem or injury, call your veterinarian. Find a veterinarian with reptile (turtle and tortoise) experience first by visiting a local herp society meeting or by calling the vets in your area and inquiring about their reptile experience and especially experience with tortoises. (Most veterinarians will have limited experience, but more and more are becoming familiar with reptile care.) The Association of Reptile and Amphibian Veterinarians (A.R.A.V.) is an organization of veterinarians that specialize in reptile and amphibian care. You can access their website at http://www.arav.com to find a qualified veterinarian in your area.

Respiratory Ailments

Respiratory problems occur when a tortoise gets chilled or is kept in sub-optimal conditions. Minor problems can be corrected with heat and a drop in humidity. If not corrected, minor problems can progress to more serious conditions such as pneumonia. Signs of a respiratory problem include labored breathing, a nasal discharge, a gaping mouth, puffy eyes, lethargy, and a loss of appetite.

To correct minor respiratory problems, increase the warmth of the enclosure with an extra heat source such as a fixture with an incandescent bulb and/or a heating pad under the enclosure. Keep the enclosure hot and dry. Bump up the temperature from 80° to 90° (27° to 32° C) and increase the hot spot from 90° to 100° F (32° to 38° C) range.

More severe cases or tortoises that do not respond to added heat will typically require a course of antibiotics. We have found Baytril® (Enrofloxacin) and Garamycin® (Gentomycin) to be effective for treating respiratory ailments in turtles and tortoises. (You will need to consult a veterinarian for treatment or to obtain antibiotic drugs.)

Injuries

Injuries occur in these active tortoises. As mentioned earlier, the males have a tendency to ram each other (and other tortoises), especially during the breeding season and throughout the year as they establish a hierarchy. This aggressive behavior can lead to limb and shell injuries. Also, accidents occasionally occur when tortoises push against fences, topple over when climbing, turn each other over, etc.

A wash of Betadine® works well to promote the healing of minor shell scrapes and injuries and kills off harmful bacteria. Be careful using Betadine® on an open wound. (The iodine solution kills much of the healthy skin that should grow and pull the wound back together.) Instead, we use sterile water to clean the wound and use an antibiotic lotion, or Silvadene® ointment to prevent

Runny eyes may point to a medical issue or may be related to excessive heat buildup on very hot days. Photo by Drew Rheinhardt.

bacteria growth in and around the wound.

Serious injuries will usually involve a visit to your veterinarian as they might require stitches, gauze wraps, or even a fiberglass patch for severe shell damage.

Parasites

External Parasites

Many wild-caught tortoises have been imported with ticks. If you find a tick on your tortoise, it should be removed right away. Ticks drain your tortoise of blood and energy, transmit diseases, and can multiply by the hundreds. To remove the tick, grasp it firmly as close to the point of attachment to the tortoise as possible, and pull it out. Avoid leaving the head of the tick imbedded in the tortoise's skin. (This rarely occurs.) There are special tick-removing tweezers available from most camping and outdoor supply stores. Place a dab of antibiotic lotion on the area where the tick was removed for a few days afterwards.

African Heartwater Disease

Importation and movement of *Geochelone sulcata*, *G. pardalis* (Leopard Tortoise), and *Kinixys belliana* (Hinge-backed Tortoise) have been banned since March 2000 when shipments from Africa were discovered that contained a sinister tropical tick. The tick (*Amblyomma* species) typically carries a parasitic microbe (*Cowdria* species). This microbe is known to kill ruminants such as antelope and water buffalo by causing their pericardium (the membrane around the heart) to fill with fluid. This microbe is only moderately dangerous in Africa but the USDA felt that it could be transmitted to hoofstock in the United States and could wipe out huge numbers of cows, sheep, goats, and deer if it were to become established. Of special concern was Florida, a tropical environment known to be especially favorable for sustaining exotic species that have escaped into the wild. The USDA passed a rule immediately restricting the transport of these three species of tortoises. Now, documents from a veterinarian are required for their transport. These documents must certify that the tortoises are free of ticks.

Internal Parasites

Imported tortoises, or those mixed with imported specimens, are often plagued by a variety of internal parasites. You can verify

Parasite ova (lower right) are seen in the fecal exams of tortoises with parasitic infestations. Photo by Barb Bonner, DVM.

an infestation if you see worms or proglottids (worm segments) in a tortoise's feces or by having a fecal check done by your veterinarian. Adult parasitic worms pass many eggs out with a tortoise's feces. These eggs can be seen under a microscope.

We use Panacur® (Fenbendazole) and Flagyl® (Metronidazole) to eliminate most parasitic infections. Panacur® works well for roundworms (nematodes) and Flagyl® works well for eliminating amoebic organisms.

Panacur® (Fenbendazole)

Panacur® is recommended for the elimination of parasitic worms.

Dosage of Panacur®
25-50 mg / kg
2 ml / kg (2.5%)

(1 kg = 2.2 pounds)

From *Understanding Reptile Parasites* by Roger Klingenberg DVM, (1993) Advanced Vivarium Systems, Inc. Mission Viejo, CA.

The easiest way to deparasitize most chelonians with Panacur® is to plaster their favorite food with it. A piece of banana or mango can be covered with the proper dosage of Panacur® and carefully fed to the tortoise. In a community situation, be sure that each individual tortoise receives a "dosed up" piece of banana or other fruit and that an eager individual doesn't snatch the food from its fellow tortoises. Watch closely and keep a Tortoise Notebook handy for jotting down information that you won't remember later. In addition, when we see a tortoise "eat" a dose of Panacur®, we dab a small splotch of acrylic paint onto its carapace. This small splotch is color-coded for 1st treatment (yellow), 2nd treatment (red), etc. In the Tortoise Notebook we note the date, time, food accepted, estimated dosage, tortoise's name or id number, sex of tortoise, etc. After 3-4 treatments, the infected tortoise's fecal sample is rechecked for presence of parasites or their ova. The veterinarian's printout is added to this tortoise's page in the Tortoise Notebook.

Flagyl® (Metronidazole)

Flagyl® is recommended for the elimination of amoebic parasites and gram-negative bacterial organisms.

Flagyl® is available as a liquid and as a 250 mg tablet or a 500 mg tablet.

Dosage of Flagyl® (Metronidazole)
25-50 mg / kg
3 ml / kg (2.3%)

(1 kg = 2.2 pounds)

From *Understanding Reptile Parasites* by Roger Klingenberg DVM, (1993) Advanced Vivarium Systems, Inc. Mission Viejo, CA.

We suggest that each of your tortoises that lives outdoors, even those that are captive-hatched, be tested for parasites once a year. Simply bottle up a small fecal sample, note which tortoise "deposited it" in your Tortoise Notebook, and take it to your local veterinarian for a check. (Don't put the sample in alcohol or other preservative; keeping it dry or in water is best.)

Become knowledgeable about parasites, especially parasitic worms. Use good husbandry and hygiene to avoid infection and reinfection. Look for potential problems and stop them before they cause you heartache.

Ivermectin® and Tortoises

Do not use Ivermectin® on tortoises. This wormer, commonly available at agriculture supply companies and used by many veterinarians will remove parasites from horses and cattle efficiently, but it will kill tortoises. Do not use it.

Poisoning

In outdoor enclosures, overlying trees and nearby plants often shed leaves and flowers into the turtles' enclosure. Turtles will usually eat this vegetation. If any of this foliage is toxic, problems including paralysis and drowning can occur.

* SOME COMMON POISONOUS PLANTS

Avocado (leaves)
Bird of Paradise
Bottlebrush
Caladium
Calla Lilly
Common Privet
Cone Flower
Daisy
Day Lily
Dieffenbachia
Dogwood
Dracaena
English Ivy
Eucalyptus
Foxglove
Hemlock
Impatiens
Iris
Ivy
Jasmine
Larkspur
Lily of the Valley
Mesquite
Milkweed
Mistletoe
Morning Glory
Mushrooms (some wild species)
Nandina
Oak
Oleander

Peach (leaves, pit)
Peony
Periwinkle
Philodendron
Poinsettia
Poison Ivy
Poison Oak
Poison Sumac
Pokeweed
Potato (leaves)
Pothos Ivy
Privet
Rhododendron
Rhubarb
Sage
Sago Palm
Schefflera
Snapdragon
Sweet Pea
Sweet Potato
Tomato (leaves)
Tulip
Verbena
Vinca
Walnut hulls
Wisteria
Yew
Yucca

* This list was compiled from conversations with various turtle and tortoise keepers, from the reference below, and from personal experience. A very good list is available from the California Turtle and Tortoise Club's Poisonous Plant List printed in the **Tortuga Gazette 28(1): 8-10, January 1992** and found on their website at **http://www.tortoise.org**. Their list is based on the University of California Irvine's Regional Poison Center list of plants that are toxic or potentially toxic to humans.

Other Health Issues

Pyramiding

Pyramiding is when a tortoise shows abnormal growth on its carapace, making it look bumpy. This condition is caused when a tortoise eats a diet that is too high in protein and too low in calcium. It is seen in captive sulcatas when a tortoise is fed solely on commercial diets or even when a tortoise eats too much of a good diet. There is some disagreement on the damaging effects of pyramiding . . . but not too much disagreement. Some

Pyramiding of the shell can be moderate, as in this specimen, to quite severe.
Photo by Russ Gurley.

African Spurred Tortoises

keepers say that pyramiding is simply the sign of a healthy, well-fed captive tortoise. Most breeders (including us) however, believe that pyramiding is aberrant and is characteristic of unnatural growth. No long-term studies have been completed, but it is well-documented that captive tortoises that have unnatural growth and especially those that are obese, exhibit kidney and liver problems that significantly shorten their lives.

Irregular Scutes

Occasionally, young sulcatas are seen with irregular scutes. This abnormality can range from barely noticeable to quite severe. These "spiderweb" scutes are caused when an egg has been incubated too hot either accidentally or by a breeder trying to rush the incubation time. Though unnatural-looking, these tortoises usually do not exhibit other health problems.

Lumpy Jaws

A sulcata's jaw should be strong, solid, and symmetrical. There should be no bumps and no overgrowth of the beak. Both are signs of poor nutrition or a poor captive environment.

Soft Shell

Soft shell is a more severe malady arising from lack of direct sunlight and calcium. This happens when a tortoise's blood stream shaves calcium from its bones and its shell to meet the calcium needs of the muscular and other body systems, leaving the tortoise's shell soft and pliable. This condition can be corrected by the addition of calcium and vitamin supplements on its food and by the addition of plenty of natural sunlight.

Most health-related problems can be prevented or resolved quickly if your tortoises are kept hot and dry in a proper captive environment. Be sure to offer them plenty of grass for food and occasionally add high-quality calcium and vitamins to a mixed, finely chopped salad. Offer a proper substrate and keep their enclosure clean.

Chapter EIGHT: BREEDING

The large male African Spurred Tortoise will use his considerable bulk to immobilize the female during mating. Photo by Rusty Mills.

In captivity, African Spurred Tortoises are very prolific. In nature, a female typically lays only one clutch of eggs per year. The hatching of this nest coincides with the onset of the rainy season and the resulting growth of plants for the hatchlings. In captivity, a large well-fed female can lay multiple clutches of from 10 to 20 eggs each year. Fertility is usually high and a sulcata breeder can find himself or herself with lots of healthy babies each year. If an "outlet" is developed, the babies can be sold quite easily. The money raised from this tortoise breeding operation can be used to pay for supplies, to pay for the big food bill, and to purchase other tortoises.

The dilemma then arises . . . Are there too many African Spurred Tortoises around? Like pythons and other over-sized pet reptiles, we often ask ourselves, 'Are these wonderful animals

Large sulcatas will often lead a peaceful existence in spacious enclosures that offer plenty of browse, shelter, and fresh water. Photo by Bob Ashley.

becoming disposable pets once they get too big? When they get big will people dump them?' The question is being answered now and unfortunately that is what is happening. There are even reports of African Spurred Tortoises being turned loose into desert tortoise habitat in the fragile deserts of southern California and Arizona.

Please do not ever release an animal into the wild. There are potential dangers to native wildlife including disease transmission, competition for food and habitat, and other damage that is poorly understood.

Be a conscientious breeder. Enjoy your tortoises and don't feel pressed to breed them and produce lots of babies. Be mindful that breeding tortoises at a young age can also be unhealthy for them.

The anal notch of females is flared and rounded to allow the passage of eggs during laying. Photo by Rusty Mills.

The anal notch of the male is flatter and wider to allow the tail to freely move during copulation. Photo by Rusty Mills.

A comparison of two large African Spurred Toroises. The male (left) has a wider and flatter anal notch, longer tail, flared back carapace, and a noticeable concavity to his plastron while the female (right) has a rounded anal notch, shorter tail, and less concave plastron. Photo by Rusty Mills.

The same pair showing the front enlarged gulars of the male (right) and the shorter gulars of the female (left). Photo by Rusty Mills.

Sexing

Though it is difficult to determine visually in a young tortoise, at about 12" to 14" (typically 3-4 years) your sulcata will begin showing some signs of its sex. At this size it is usually 6" to 8" (2-3 years) away from breeding, but you will have an idea of what the sex of your tortoise is and your ability to produce baby sulcatas in the future.

Females

Females usually mature at 17" to 18" which usually translates to 7 to 8 years of healthy growth in captivity. Female sulcatas have a short tail. The shape of the anal notch is comparatively wide and rounded to allow the passage of eggs.

Males

Male sulcatas usually mature at 15" to 16" which is usually indicative of 5 to 6 years of healthy growth in captivity. Male sulcatas have a longer tail that usually folds to the side. The opening of the anal notch is quite wide. Male African Spurred Tortoises, like other male tortoises, have a fairly deep concavity to the plastron.

Courtship and Pre-mating Behavior

Aggression

Aggression exhibited by male African Spurred Tortoises during the breeding season is common and ocasionally violent. As they mature, males will begin ramming and mounting other males to assert their dominance. During the breeding time, overly aggressive males will occasionally attack other tortoises, pets, and even people, ramming them with their gular projections with incredible force.

Female sulcatas sometimes exhibit aggressive behaviors as well. They

Aggression related to mating can involve chasing and ramming. Photo by Rusty Mills.

When tortoises ram each other, there is a chance that a smaller tortoise may be overturned, sometimes leading to deadly consequences. Photo by Rusty Mills.

will shove males to prevent unwanted advances and will often ram other tortoises that come too close to their "secure" resting space. This is common when the females are gravid (have eggs) and especially when egg-laying is imminent.

Mating

The large male sulcata mounts the female with little or no courtship behavior other than "the chase". A successful breeding male typically outweighs the female by many, many pounds. The extreme size discrepancy allows the male to weigh down the female and immobilize her. This mating practice is also seen in Galapagos Tortoises and Aldabra Tortoises. Smaller male sulcatas are usually unsuccessful in breeding as they are dislodged, pushed away, or carried off by a larger female. During copulation, the male will usually raise and lower himself, scraping the female's carapace. There is also usually some tail stimulation and vocalization during mating.

Vocalization

While mating, male sulcatas often emit a loud quacking sound. This vocalization is common in a variety of the world's tortoises from small to large.

Egg-laying

In the wild, most breeding and egg-laying revolves around the rainy season (when it exists). Typically, a female will lay a single clutch of eggs just before the rainy season. The eggs incubate for around 200 days and the hatchlings emerge just before the next rainy season. This "system" allows the young tortoises to take advantage of the new and abundant plant growth. In captivity, mating activity for African Spurred Tortoises can begin in cooler months as spring approaches and typically lasts throughout the warmer months.

Within about 30 days of mating, the female will begin showing signs of imminent egg-laying. As this time approaches, the female begins to eat less and becomes restless, pacing the enclosure. Over a period of 5-10 days she may dig as many as

Female sulcatas are typically very good about digging a deep nest and burying their eggs. This female laid a clutch of egg late in the year in the cypress mulch of her winter quarters. Photo by Rusty Mills.

3-4 test holes. When ready to lay eggs, she will dig the actual nest, which is usually a long and arduous feat. She will dig with both front and back legs, excavating a 24" diameter hole that is roughly 12" deep. Within this hole, she will dig a smaller (8" diameter by 10" deep) inner hole for the egg chamber. If the ground is hard, she will urinate as she digs to soften the earth. After digging and laying from 10 to 20 eggs inside, she will take 1-2 hours to cover the nest. She will cover the nest efficiently and hide it well, so be diligent and watch for digging activity so you don't lose the opportunity to remove and incubate the eggs. Removal of the eggs is best done in the first few days to prevent injury to the developing embryos.

Small female sulcatas will typically lay smaller clutches of only 10 to 12 eggs. A larger female will usually lay 20 to 25 eggs. In areas with warm springs and summers, sulcatas can lay three or four clutches every 30 to 50 days. In hotter environments, a well-fed female sulcata can lay as many as six clutches of eggs each year. Often, the first clutch will have a lower fertility rate than later clutches.

Chapter NINE: The Eggs and Incubation

African Spurred Tortoise eggs incubating.   Photo by Bob Ashley.

The Eggs

Healthy sulcata eggs are round with fairly brittle shells and are usually in the 1.5" to 2" and 25 to 30 gram range, depending on the individual female tortoise.

Once you've discovered the eggs and removed them from the nest, you have a couple of options. You can keep it simple and incubate the eggs in a plastic shoe box in a dark, warm area such as a closet or you can place them in a commercial or homemade incubator.

Sulcata eggs typically do not go through a diapause (resting period), but they have an interesting habit of hatching over an extended period of time. Eggs from a single clutch laid within a few minutes of each other can hatch over a two-week period.

A diligent breeder will keep track of laying females so that it is much easier to find and carefully remove the eggs for incubation. Courtesy of the Captive Bred Wildlife Foundation. Photo by Bob Ashley.

Digging the Eggs

The newly laid eggs can be carefully dug up with your hands or a small shovel. As you reach the eggs in the nest, carefully brush away the substrate and remove the eggs one by one. As you gently remove them, mark the top of each egg with an X in pencil as you move them to the container in which they will be incubated. This will let you establish a "top" to the egg so you don't roll or rotate the egg later. Many breeders use vermiculite as an incubation medium. We use a mixture of ½ vermiculite, ¼ dampened sand, and ¼ peat moss. We use the vermiculite-sand-peat mixture for a couple of reasons: 1. This is a "natural" mix 2. We have found that most turtle eggs incubated in this mixture with some sand and peat have a higher rate of hatching. It appears that the acidity of the peat slowly erodes the surface of the eggs as they incubate and this allows easier "pipping" (emergence) by the hatchlings. This mixture is initially dampened with purified or distilled water to the point that it clumps but does not drip water out of a tightly squeezed handful. Make sure there is no excess water in the bottom of the container. Make a depression with your thumb or a spoon in the damp substrate and gently place the egg into the depression. Carefully push the substrate up around the egg, leaving only the top slightly exposed. After all of the eggs have been removed from the nest and have been placed into the incubation container, we cover the eggs with a layer of very lightly dampened sand or vermiculite to hold in the moisture.

Temperature, Humidity, and Time for Incubation

Sulcata eggs, like sulcata tortoises, are very forgiving. We recommend an incubation temperature of 86° F (30° C) and 75% to 85% humidity. At this temperature the tortoises will begin hatching in roughly 90 days but hatching can take place in the following week or two. Lower incubation temperatures will extend the time and hotter temperatures can speed up the hatching by a week or even two.

Be observant - Eggs incubated too cold will fail to develop and those incubated too hot may kill the developing the embryos.

Shelf Method

Eggs can be incubated on a shelf in a dark closet. They should be watched closely to monitor humidity and temperature. They

In a warm room, sulcata eggs can be successfully incubated in their incubation containers resting on a shelf. Photo by Bob Ashley.

A typical incubation box (with the lid removed) with the eggs partially buried in slightly dampened vermiculite. Photo by Bob Ashley.

should be warm as eggs incubated too cool will not develop. When incubated in this manner, eggs will typically take longer to hatch, as it will no doubt be cooler than in an incubator. On a shelf system, you usually remove the possibility of eggs over-heating – an occasional occurrence when using an electric incubator. Also, some breeders feel that the natural daily fluctuation of temperatures in this shelf system gives them more vigorous and healthy hatchlings.

Incubators

There are a variety of incubators on the market. They can be purchased from reptile supply companies, some pet stores, farm and garden stores, and on the internet. We have found that Hovabator® incubators are inexpensive and work well. Make sure to set up the incubator for a few days to make sure that the proper temperature is established before the eggs are placed inside. Take the shoe boxes containing the eggs and place them inside the incubator. Make careful notes in your Tortoise Notebook. Include the date the eggs were laid, the temperature and the humidity inside the incubator, dates eggs hatched, etc.

We add a thermometer / hygrometer (TAYLOR model 1452)

Small, inexpensive incubators can be used to hatch single clutches of sulcata eggs. Photo by Russ Gurley.

in the top of each incubation container. This allows us to monitor the proper incubation temperature and humidity and lets us keep notes of the daily temperature and humidity. These notes can be useful when your tortoise lays again. Also it lets you share with other tortoise breeders the conditions which were successful and those which were not successful.

Good Eggs and Bad Eggs

As the tortoise embryo develops within the egg, a number of changes occur. In most tortoise eggs, there is a noticeable change in the external appearance of the egg. The egg typically darkens and loses the pinkish tint seen in a newly laid egg. "Chalking" is the appearance of a white opacity to the developing egg. This can appear as a band around the middle of the egg, chalkiness at the ends of the eggs, or an overall change from pinkish or yellowish to white. This "chalking" occurs when the calcium moves from the egg's shell to the developing embryo within. This is a sign that the egg is fertile and that the embryo is developing.

If an egg shows no darkening or change in color, it is most likely infertile. However, you should never discard eggs as even eggs that have discolored, become dented, and even those that have small cracks or slight damage have produced healthy baby turtles.

As the end of the incubation period for the tortoise egg nears, carbon dioxide builds up within the egg and the young tortoise is forced out of the egg and "pipping", the first stage of hatching occurs.

"Pipping" and the "Egg Tooth"

Hatching occurs when the baby tortoise cuts or "pecks" its way out of the egg. This process is aided by the presence of a caruncle or "egg tooth" on the tip of its snout. This structure varies from species to species, but is typically a small, hard projection. The baby African Spurred Tortoise forces a hole or slice in the egg with the "egg tooth" and then the baby tortoise will use his legs, head, or mouth to widen the opening in the egg. Once it is able to breathe the outside air, it may rest within the egg for an hour up to several days, gaining strength, absorbing the remainder of its yolk sac, and preparing for the struggles that lay ahead. Within a few days of emerging from the egg, the "egg tooth" falls off.

Be patient. Babies from the same clutch can hatch over a 14 day period.

Upon hatching, make sure the baby tortoise's yolk sac has been completely absorbed. If the yolk sac is abnormally large, you have a couple of choices: 1. You can leave the tortoise in the warmth of the incubator. In a couple of days, the sac should be completely absorbed. In some areas, small "carrion" flies or gnats will invade an incubator, drawn by the albumen and other tissue in the newly vacated eggs. The larvae of these flies will attack recently hatched babies and can kill them within a matter of hours. If you feel that the incubator is unsafe during this time and your hatchlings need further absorption of their yolk sac, you can remove the empty eggs and replace the substrate with new,

---

A hatching sulcata uses its egg tooth to chip its way out of the egg. The yolk sac is visible underneath this hatchling. Photo by Bill Love.

clean substrate.   2. Another choice is to move the hatchlings into a small plastic tub or shoe box with clean, lightly dampened paper towel in the bottom. Let them rest quietly in the safety and warmth of the tub. In a couple of days, the sac should be absorbed completely. If they hatch out with the yolk sac absorbed, and only a small button showing, set them up in their first home.

Chapter TEN: HATCHLINGS

Hatchling tortoises can be set up in a simple plastic tub with newspaper or paper towel in the bottom. This enclosure is easy to clean and maintain while watching the first few weeks of the tortoises' life. Photo by Bob Ashley.

Hatchling sulcatas emerge from the egg at about 2 ½" long and weighing a little over an ounce (28 to 32 grams). They emerge from the egg a little folded up, but seem to inflate into a normal appearing hatchling within a day or two of hatching. They typically have a pale yellow carapace with dark brown seams. Within a few days to as much as a week, they begin the mission of eating, exploring, and growing. They are active during feeding time and spend much of the day resting near the hot spot in their enclosure.

A Baby Sulcata's First Home

The first enclosure for a small tortoise can be a terrarium in the 10 to 20 gallon range. We have found 20-gallon long aquariums to be ideal. The length of these aquariums (30" l x 12" w x 12" h) gives you a good space to establish a temperature gradient within the enclosure. By placing a clamp type fixture with a 100 watt

The extra length of a 20-gallon long aquarium can make an ideal home for a young sulcata. Photo by Russ Gurley.

(spot) T-Rex Active UV-heat bulb® over one end, the keeper can establish the required 90° to 95° F (32° to 35° C) basking spot and UV rays that are essential for these growing babies. Maintain the other end in the 80° to 85° F (27° to 29° C) range.

Tubs

If you hatch out many babies, you may choose to raise them in blanket boxes, sweater boxes, or even small cement-mixing tubs. These tubs are inexpensive and make good enclosures for small tortoises. They can be stacked on a rack system, allowing you to keep many tortoises in a relatively small space.

Substrate

Breeders use a variety of substrates for young sulcatas. Cypress mulch, grass clippings, and rabbit food are the most commonly used. These are safe, easy to clean, and inexpensive.   Paper towels are also good because they are inexpensive. When the towel gets soiled, it can be easily removed and replaced with new.   A sand and peat mixture is an inexpensive and natural substrate.

Heat

As mentioned above, high heat and aridity with a temperature gradient is necessary to keep these tortoises healthy. We maintain our babies in an enclosure that stays 80° to 85° F (27° to 29° C) throughout the day and that has a basking spot that stays at 95° F (35° C). During the winter we add a reptile heating pad on the low setting underneath the "hot" end of their vivarium to maintain the proper temperature.

Lighting

We use shop light fixtures with high-quality UVB bulbs and a T-Rex Active UV-heat® bulb above all of our indoor turtles and tortoises. We use a 12 hours daylight / 12 hours dark schedule for most of the year until they are 4-5 years old. It is then that we begin to cool them slightly for winter conditioning. At this time, the light is changed from 8-10 hours of daylight and 14-16 hours of dark.

Shelter

Add a piece of cork bark, drift wood, a stable pile of rocks, or a commercial shelter to make an interesting and exciting tortoise enclosure.

First Foods

We feed our hatchling and young sulcatas every other day.

First foods for a hatchling sulcata should include grass, dandelions, clover, strips of *Opuntia* cactus (whenever possible) and a finely chopped salad consisting of a variety of leafy plants including kale, romaine lettuce, redleaf lettuce, greenleaf lettuce, cabbage, zucchini, broccoli, alfalfa, and others.

Remember, LOW PROTEIN is the goal. You want to maintain variety and prevent pyramiding and obesity.

If you ever have a baby tortoise that is a finicky eater, offer it strawberry, a piece of red bell pepper, or banana. These seem to stimulate non-feeding tortoises with their color or smell. Once feeding, switch any finicky eaters to the recommended healthy diet.

OUTDOORS

As much as possible, place your baby sulcatas outside to reap the benefits of direct sunlight. Obviously, for small sulcatas, extreme care must be taken that the outdoor enclosure is secure. In some areas, a strong top will be necessary. Add some shelter and shady spots inside the enclosure.

This secure top will help avoid predation by dogs, cats, raccoons, opossums, rats, and birds. (All of these are known predators of baby tortoises.) You can avoid most problems by adding a sturdy cover made of wood and hardware cloth. This cover will keep all but the smallest predators out and allow helpful UVB rays in. Baby sulcatas typically feed better outside and as they roam their enclosure, they get exercise and have access to additional food items.

Baby sulcatas show their distinctive personalities almost immediately. They are

Creative outdoor enclosures for small tortoises can be created with landscape timbers arranged around a shade tree. Photo by Russ Gurley.

As soon as they are feeding well and their yolk sacs are completely absorbed, young sulcatas can be moved outside to enjoy larger spaces and natural sunlight. Photo by Russ Gurley.

alert, inquisitive, and extremely docile. They will eagerly eat small pieces of greens from their keeper's hands and roam out to investigate when you come near them. Within a very short time they will transform themselves from newly hatched strangers and into members of the family.

Sulcatas spend a great deal of time digging and wallowing in the damp soil of their enclosures. Photo by Russ Gurley.

The thick scales of the front legs provide protection for the head when the legs are pulled into the shell. Photo by Russ Gurley.

African Spurred Tortoises

There are a few strains of albino sulcatas in captive breeding programs. Courtesy of Reptile Industries. Photo by Bob Ashley.

The Ivory Tortoise is a color form of sulcata that remains pale yellow with dark eyes. Courtesy of Riparian Farms. Photo by Jerry Fife.

RED-FOOTED TORTOISES
Geochelone carbonaria

Red-footed Tortoises are colorful, docile, and hardy when cared for properly.
Photo by Bob Ashley.

Distribution: Panama and Colombia to Paraguay, Brazil, and Argentina. Introduced into the West Indies.

Habitat: Red-footed Tortoises are found in tropical and humid forest areas. They live in the underbrush and forage for fallen fruit, plant growth, and will even eat carrion.

Indoor Enclosures: Most keepers use glass terrariums for small or medium sized Red-footed Tortoises. For young tortoises, we suggest a 20-gallong long terrarium (20" l x 12" w x 12" h). Medium tortoises will need a 40 breeder terrarium or larger. Keepers can also use plastic tubs, wooden cages, and other enclosures, but glass terrariums are easy to find at the local pet store and they come in a variety of sizes. We suggest taping paper on the back and sides of glass terrariums to keep the young tortoise from constantly trying to walk through the clear glass.

Young Red-foots are often more colorful than their adult counterparts.   Photo by Russ Gurley.

Of course, as the tortoise grows, it will need larger and larger enclosures. A pair of adult Red-foots will require an enclosure that is at least 4' wide x 6' long.

The substrate for Red-foots can be a mixture of ½ sand and ½ peat moss. A layer of cypress mulch can be placed over the top of the substrate to help hold in moisture. The addition of piles of dry leaves, hay, and plants in pots can add to the natural look of a Red-foot enclosure.

A variety of shelters can be offered to give the young Red-foot a feeling of security. We add large pieces of curved cork bark, large banana leaves, piles of hay, or grass clippings for the tortoises to use as shelter. The shelter should be located at the cooler end of the enclosure and not directly under the heat-emitting lamps.

Water should be offered in a large flat saucer. This can be a cat litter pan sunk into the substrate (make sure the tortoise can climb in and out easily) or a large plastic saucer which is normally placed under a potted plant. These can be easily cleaned and sterilized once a week or as needed.

The most successful Red-foot breeders are located in warm climates and they keep their breeder tortoises outside all year. Courtesy of Reptile Industries. Photo by Bob Ashley.

Heat should be provided using a heat-emitting bulb in a clamp-type fixture over the enclosure. Ideally, a keeper will hang a fixture overhead that will hold the bulb and keep it about 12" above the surface of the substrate. Most of these bulbs get very hot and so should be kept in a fixture with a ceramic base. The heat-emitting bulbs should provide a basking spot of 90° F (32° C) at one end of the enclosure. The heat in this area will allow the Red-foot to bask and to digest its food properly.

Most keepers will also place a shop light fixture overhead that is fitted with one or two UV-emitting bulbs. These can be found at your pet store or on-line from a variety of sources. UVB-heat bulbs® from T-Rex products and Zoomed Reptisun® bulbs will provide UV radiation to the enclosure. This UVB is necessary for Vitamin D3 synthesis, which allows the tortoises to properly use calcium and to carry on metabolism.

Outdoor Enclosures: Of course, all tortoises benefit from being kept outdoors for all or part of their lives. They received doses of UVB radiation, environmental heat, and of course enjoy a connection to the grass, plants, and soil found in outdoor pens. Outdoor enclosures should offer shelter from heat, a secure place

Outdoor enclosures should offer plenty of shelters to make the tortoises feel more secure. Courtesy of Linda Putnam. Photo by Russ Gurley.

to rest, and a water source. We feed our outdoor tortoises three times a week and at their leisure they can eat some of their favorite grasses, fruits, and vegetables within the enclosure. A keeper must be very diligent to make sure that outdoor enclosures are escape-proof and predator-proof.

Red-foots require warm, humid environments and so keepers living in arid areas will need to offer mud wallows or will need to turn on the water sprinkler once a day, especially during midday heat.

Feeding: Red-foots are omnivorous, eating both animal and plant material in nature. In captivity they will feed eagerly on a mixed salad of fruits and vegetables every other day. They should be fed some higher protein items once or twice a week. Most Red-foots will eagerly feed on dead mice and dead chicks, but some keepers prefer to feed them a high-quality commercial food once a week. Mazuri Tortoise Diet® and Zupreem Primate Diet® ("Monkey Biscuits") are great supplements to the Red-foot's diet.

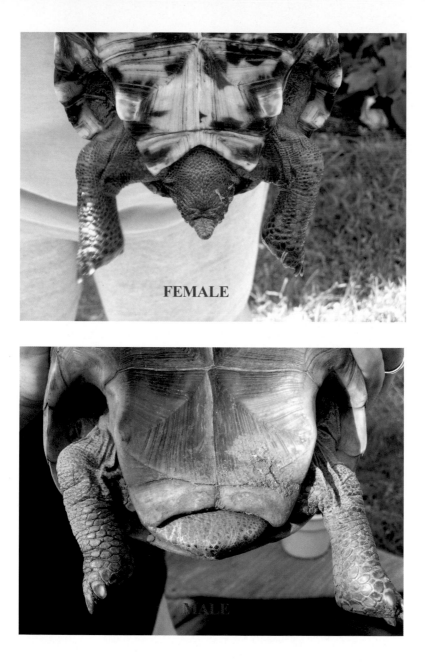

FEMALE

MALE

Breeding: A light winter cooling, followed by warm, rainy days triggers breeding in Red-footed Tortoises. Males are very eager breeders and a healthy pair can produce two to four clutches of 3 to 4 eggs each season, depending on the size of the female. It is

A healthy pair of adult Red-footed Tortoises can be quite prolific. Photo by Russ Gurley.

felt by most keepers that the addition of protein and calcium to a female Red-foot's diet is essential in having her produce clutches of healthy, viable eggs. The young Redfoots hatch out in approximately 100 days at 82° to 84° F.

Comments: Red-footed Tortoises are among the best pet tortoises. They stay relatively small (12" to 16" for most types), they are colorful, they are hardy and long-lived, and can be some of the most personable tortoises to keep as pets.

YELLOWFOOT TORTOISES
Geochelone denticulata

Yellow-foots are typically not as colorful as Red-foots, but can make wonderful pets. Photo by Russ Gurley.

Comments: Yellow-foot Tortoises are not as colorful as their kin, the Red-foots, and they have the reputation of being more delicate captives. They also grow a bit larger than Red-foots, with some specimens growing to 26" to 28". However, most specimens will only reach 14" to 16".

Distribution: Colombia and Venezuela to Bolivia, Brazil, and Trinidad

Habitat: Yellow-foot Tortoises are found in tropical and humid forest areas. They live in the underbrush and forage for fallen fruit, plant growth, and will even eat carrion.

Indoor Enclosures: The most common form of indoor accommodation for small or medium sized Yellow-foot Tortoises is a large terrarium. Keepers can use plastic tubs, wooden cages,

A large stock tank can be used to house one or two Yellow-foots indoors.
Photo by Russ Gurley.

and other enclosures, but glass terrariums are easy to find at the local pet store and they come in a variety of sizes. Of course, as the tortoise grows, it will need larger and larger enclosures. A pair of adult Yellow-foots will require an enclosure that is at least 4' wide x 6' long.

The substrate for Yellow-foots can be a mixture of ½ sand and ½ peat moss. A layer of cypress mulch should be placed over the top of the substrate to help hold in moisture. The substrate can be kept dry if a large water source is provided. This should be a shallow flower pot for small specimens and a larger tub for larger specimens. The space underneath the Yellowfoot's favorite shelter should be sprayed with water once or twice a week to keep this area damp.

A variety of shelters can be offered to give a young tortoise a feeling of security. We add large pieces of curved cork bark, large banana leaves, piles of straw or hay, or grass clippings for the tortoises to use as shelter. The shelter should be located at the cooler end of the enclosure and not directly under the heat-emitting lamps.

Heat should be provided using a heat-emitting bulb in a lamp from overhead. The heat-emitting bulbs should be provide a basking spot of 90º F (32º C) at one end of the enclosure. UVB is necessary for Vitamin D3 production.

Outdoor Enclosures: Yellow-foots benefit from being kept outdoors for all or part of their lives. They received doses of UVB radiation, environmental heat, and of course enjoy a connection to the grass, plants, and soil found in outdoor pens. Outdoor enclosures should offer shelter from heat, a secure place to rest, and a water source. Food can be offered to tortoises and can be supplemented by plantings of some of their favorite grasses, fruits, and vegetables within the enclosure. A keeper must be very diligent to make sure that outdoor enclosures are escape-proof and predator-proof.

Feeding: Yellow-foots are omnivores, eating both animal and plant material in nature. In captivity most keepers offer them a mixed salad of fruits and vegetables every other day. They should also be fed some higher protein items once or twice a week. Dead mice, Mazuri Tortoise Diet®, Zupreem Primate Diet®, and other commercial foods are also great additions to the Yellow-foot's diet.

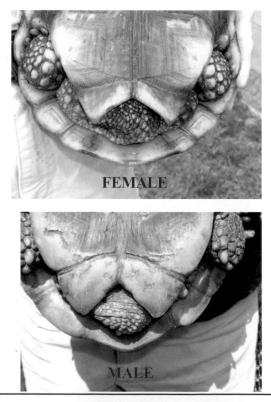

FEMALE

MALE

Breeding: A light winter cooling, followed by warm, rainy days triggers breeding in Yellow-foots. Males are typically eager breeders and a healthy pair can produce two clutches of 6 to 12 eggs each season, depending on the size of the female. These clutches are typically laid four to six weeks apart. It is felt by most keepers that the addition of protein and calcium to female Yellow-foots' diets is essential in having them produce clutches of healthy, viable eggs. The young Yellowfoots hatch in 100 to 120 days when incubated at 84° F.

Comments: Captive-hatched Yellow-foot tortoises are among the best pet tortoises. They stay relatively small (12 to 16" for most types). They are hardy and long-lived and can make wonderful pets.

* For most keepers, wild-caught Yellow-foots should be avoided. Recently imported Yellow-foots are typically stressed, dehydrated, and will harbor a variety of internal parasites.

LEOPARD TORTOISES
Geochelone pardalis

Like sulcatas, Leopard Tortoises thrive in environments and enclosures that offer hot, dry conditions. Photo by Bob Ashley.

Comments: Leopard Tortoises are beautiful black and yellow tortoises with intricate spotted patterns on their shells. They grow quite large, with many adults reaching 14" to 16". Large females of *G. p. pardalis* can reach 18" to 20" and 40 to 60 pounds, but captive specimens this large are rare.

Distribution: Most tortoise keepers acknowledge that there are two subspecies (or at least forms) of Leopard Tortoises. *Geochelone pardalis babcocki* is smaller and is found in a wide range in nature, including much of eastern Africa. The other subspecies, *Geochelone pardalis pardalis*, grows to a much larger adult size and is found in the South Africa and southern Namibia.

Habitat: Leopard Tortoises are found in hot, dry scrubland areas in southern Africa. They live in the underbrush, seeking refuge from the heat under brushy plants and other shady areas. They browse grass and plant growth.

Indoor Enclosures: The most common form of indoor accommodation for small or medium sized Leopard Tortoises is a large terrarium. Keepers can use plastic tubs, wooden cages, and other enclosures, but glass terrariums are easy to find at the local pet store and they come in a variety of sizes. Of course, as the tortoise grows, it will need larger and larger enclosures. A pair of adult Leopard Tortoises will require an enclosure that is at least 4' wide x 6' long.

The substrate for Leopards can be a mixture of ¾ sand and ¼ peat moss. A layer of grass hay can be added at one end to provide some shelter. The substrate should be kept dry as Leopard Tortoises are very sensitive to damp conditions.

Leopard Tortoises are shy and so a keeper should provide a variety of shelters to give these tortoises a feeling of security. We add large pieces of curved cork bark, large banana leaves, piles of straw or hay, etc. for the tortoises to use as shelter. The shelter should be located at the cooler end of the enclosure and not directly under the heat-emitting lamps.

Water should be offered in a flat saucer. This can be a flat dish or a plastic saucer which is normally placed under a plant pot. These can be easily cleaned and sterilized once a week or as needed.

Heat should be provided using a heat-emitting bulb in a lamp from overhead. Ideally, this heat lamp should hang just about 12" above the substrate. The heat-emitting bulb should be provide a basking spot of 90° to 95° F (32° to 35° C) at one end of the enclosure. This will provide a hot end for the tortoise to enjoy. Most keepers will also place a shop light fixture overhead that is fitted with one or two UV-emitting bulbs. These can be found at your pet store or on-line from a variety of sources. UVB-heat bulbs® from T-Rex products and Reptisun® bulbs from Zoomed will also provide UV radiation to the enclosure. This UVB is necessary for Vitamin D3 production (needed for calcium absorpion, proper muscle functioning, etc.).

During the hottest days, Leopard Tortoises should have access to shade and water. Photo by Russ Gurley.

Outdoor Enclosures: All tortoises benefit from being kept outdoors for all or part of their lives. They receive doses of UVB radiation, environmental heat, and of course enjoy a connection to the grass, plants, and soil found in outdoor pens. Outdoor enclosures should offer shelter from heat, a secure place to rest, and a water source. Food can be offered to tortoises and can be supplemented by plantings of some of their favorite grasses, fruits, and vegetables within the enclosure. A keeper must be very diligent to make sure that outdoor enclosures are escape-proof and predator-proof.

Leopard Tortoises require warm, dry environments and so keepers living in humid areas should be very careful about keeping Leopard Tortoises outdoors. Living on the damp ground will cause serious medical problems with Leopard Tortoises.

Feeding: Leopard Tortoises should be fed a diet that is very high in fiber. They will feed eagerly on a mixed salad of greens and vegetables each day, but a keeper should try to offer as much grass, hay, dandelions, leaves, and *Opuntia* cactus pads as possible. A sprinkle of calcium should be offered on the salad every few times. For optimal health, they should be fed fruits only sparingly or not at all. We offer our Leopards some melon, apple, and other fruits during the hot summers, but only once every ten days to two weeks. Leopard Tortoises should not be fed any dog food or cat food and commercial foods only very seldom as they are prone to renal problems and medical issues related to high protein diets.

Breeding: A light winter cooling, followed by hot days triggers breeding in Leopard Tortoises. Sometimes pairs take several

Young Leopard Tortoises should be soaked in shallow, tepid water once a week to ensure that they are drinking and clearing their digestive systems. Photo by Bob Ashley.

years to "bond" and until this occurs, females will often refuse the male's attempts to mate. A healthy, active pair can produce two clutches of 10 to 20 eggs each season. It is felt by most keepers that the addition of protein and calcium to female Leopards' diets is essential in having them produce clutches of healthy, viable eggs. Eggs hatch in as many as 150 days when incubated in the 82° to 86° F range of temperatures.

Comments: Leopard Tortoises are among the most beautiful pet tortoises. They are very shy when small, but will become more and more outgoing as they get used to their keeper's activities. Captive-hatched specimens are quite hardy as long as their husbandry requirements are met.

RUSSIAN or CENTRAL ASIAN TORTOISES
Testudo horsfieldii

Healthy Russian Tortoises are heavy and bright-eyed. Photo by Bob Ashley.

Comments: Russian Tortoises have been imported in large numbers in recent years from the Ukraine. Even as imported specimens, they are usually hardy, stay small (5" to 8"), and tolerate a wide range of conditions, including cold winters outdoors. Captive-hatched specimens make excellent pets.

Distribution: Russian Tortoises range from China to Uzbekistan and Kazakhstan in dry, arid habitats.

Habitat: Russian Tortoises live in areas with hot, dry summers and cold winters. In most of their range they live in burrows that they dig or they will modify abandoned animal burrows to fit their needs.

Indoor Enclosures: The most common form of indoor accommodation for small or medium sized Russian Tortoises is a glass

Russian Tortoises are incredible diggers and several tortoises may take up residence in the same burrow. Photo by Bob Ashley.

terrarium. Keepers can use plastic tubs, wooden cages, and other enclosures, but glass terrariums are easy to find at the local pet store and they come in a variety of sizes. A 20-long is ideal for small Russian Tortoises and larger specimens can be kept comfortably in a 40 breeder terrarium. Of course, as the tortoise grows, it will need larger and larger enclosures. A pair of adult Russian Tortoises will require an enclosure that is at least 2' wide x 4' long. Adult males are very aggressive towards each other and so a keeper must either keep one male with one (or multiple) females, or must provide a large enclosure with plenty of shelters in the form of rock piles, and other areas in which males can separate themselves from each other.

The substrate for Russians can be a mixture of ½ sand and ½ peat moss. A layer of cypress mulch can be placed over the top of the substrate. The substrate should be kept dry.

A variety of shelters can be offered to give the tortoise a feeling of security. We add large pieces of curved cork bark, piles of straw, sturdy piles of rocks, and other shelters. The shelter should be located at the cooler end of the enclosure and not directly under the heat-emitting lamps.

Water should be offered in a flat saucer, such as a plastic saucer which is normally placed under a plant pot. These can be easily cleaned and sterilized once a week or as needed.

Heat should be provided using a heat-emitting bulb in a lamp from overhead. The heat-emitting bulbs should be provide a basking spot of 90° to 95° F (32° to 35° C) at one end of the enclosure. This will provide a hot end to the tank. These bulbs can be found at your pet store or on-line from a variety of sources. UVB-emitting bulb should also be placed over the enclosure.

Outdoor Enclosures: Russian Tortoises do very well in outdoor enclosures in most areas of the United States. They enjoy warm days, but must have a shelter for them to escape the hottest afternoons. They can take cooler temperatures down into the 30s and 40s F as long as they are given an area in which they can dig down into the substrate. This area should be covered with a deep layer of straw, grass clippings, mulch and even compost to hold in some heat during the coldest days. If a keeper is unsure whether their area gets too cold for Russian Tortoises, we suggest allowing them a cooling period of a month or two in a more moderately cool area such as a garage or base-ment. They should be allowed to reach 45 to 55° F for a period of one to two months. If they are kept warmer than this, their metabolism will remain too

Outdoor Russian Tortoise enclosures should offer access to sunlight and shelters. Photo by Russ Gurley.

high and they may die during this time.

Russian Tortoises are incredible burrowers and can quickly dig under and out of an enclosure. Care must be taken to prevent this from happening.

Feeding: Russian Tortoises will feed eagerly on grasses and mixed salads of vegetables every other day. They should be fed dandelion, clover, and dark green lettuces as often as possible. They can be fed fruit, but only sparingly. Mazuri Tortoise Diet and other commercial foods can

A Russian Tortoise enjoying a slice of zuchini squash. Photo by Drew Rheinhardt.

be used to supplement the Russian Tortoise's diet, but we suggest you feed these foods only once or twice a month.

Breeding: A winter cooling, followed by warm, rainy days

Russian Tortoises are cold hardy, long-lived, and can be quite personable. If cared for properly, they are excellent pets. Photo by Russ Gurley.

triggers breeding in Russian Tortoises. These tortoises tend to be very aggressive during the mating season. A keeper needs to be observant during the Spring and make sure that the pushing and shoving does not get too violent as injuries during this time can be moderate to severe. Males are very eager breeders and a healthy pair usually produce two to three clutches of 2 to 4 eggs each year. Eggs will hatch in 80 to 90 days at 86° F. Female Russian Tortoises should be given extra supplementation in the form of calcium and vitamins when they are in the egg-laying season.

Comments: Russian Tortoises are among the best pet tortoises. They stay relatively small (4" to 6") and are active and alert. They are not the most beautiful tortoise being kept, but they are very hardy.

THE FUTURE

From their first appearance in captivity, African Spurred Tortoises captured the hearts of tortoise keepers. These giants with their beautiful sandy tan color, intelligent eyes, and inquisitive personalities were immediately a big hit!

Now, ten years later, they have become the most commonly kept pet tortoise in the world.

Despite the immediate fascination, some keepers discover right away that African Spurred Tortoises are too much for them to handle. These tortoises get too big for most people. For others, these tortoises have been worth modifying their yards, enlarging their grocery bills, and changing their daily routines.

Those just beginning to keep tortoises have to discover if sulcatas are right for them. The situation is very similar to hobbyists who consider large pythons, giant lizards, and venomous snakes. They can be advised and informed and despite a wealth of information from books, articles, and websites, they have to find out for themselves if these tortoises are right for them.

Please do not dump unwanted tortoises into natural environments, even if the natural habitat near you seems ideal for tortoises. The results can be disasterous for that habitat and will most certainly lead to regulations restricting our ability to keep pet reptiles. If you decide to move your tortoise on to another situation, take a little time to find a legitimate adoption organization for turtles and tortoises, especially large tortoises. Find organizations such as the Turtle and Tortoise Preservation Group and Turtle Homes that specialize in large, naturalistic environments for their animals and that have a network of keepers and breeders with which to place tortoises. We encourage you to join a local turtle and tortoise club or herpetological society. Read, explore, and visit with keepers and breeders in your area to find out what works best.

We hope that through this book you will understand a little more about your tortoise and be able to give it a wonderful captive environment. This environment should revolve around proper care and a daily life that keeps the tortoise both healthy and stimulated. Keep in mind that in today's world with its emphasis on technology, expansion, and fast-paced routines, these tortoises slow us down and keep us connected to the natural world.

SUGGESTED READING

Alderton, D. 1988. Turtles & Tortoises of the World. Facts on File. New York.

Bartlett, R. D. and P. Bartlett. 1996. Turtles and Tortoises: A Complete Pet Owner's Manual. Barron's Educational Series, Inc. Hauppauge, N.Y.

Corton, M. 2000. A Beginner's Guide to Leopard and Other South African Tortoises. Carapace Press. England.

Devaux, B. 2000. La tortue qui pleure (The crying tortoise) *Geochelone sulcata* (Miller; 1779). Chelonii vol. 1. SOPTOM. France.

Ernst, C.H. and R. W. Barbour. 1989. Turtles of the World. Smithsonian Institution Press.

Fedorchuck, W. 1999-2000. "African Spurred Tortoise Profile and Maintenance Guide" (On-line). Accessed at http://www.tortoiseaid.org/sulcata.html.

Flower, S.S. 1928. Examination of a living specimen of the great African tortoise, (*Testudo sulcata*). Proceedings of the Zoological Society of London. 1928:654.

Gurley, R. 2003. The African Spurred Tortoise, *Geochelone sulcata*, In Captivity. Taxon Media. Lanesboro, MN.

Harrold, A. 2001. *Geochelone sulcata* (On-line), Animal Diversity Web. Accessed August 01, 2005 at http://animaldiversity.ummz.umich.edu/site/accounts/information/Geochelone_sulcata.html.

Highfield, A. 1996. Practical Encyclopedia of Keeping and Breeding Tortoises and Freshwater Tortoises. Carapace Press. England.

Highfield, A. 2000. The Turtle and Tortoise Feeding Manual. Carapace Press. England.

Highfield, A. 2002. Understanding Reptile Lighting Systems. Tortoise Trust website - http://www.tortoisetrust.org/articles/lighting.html.

Kaplan, M. 1996. Sulcata Tortoises - African Spurred Tortoises, *Geochelone sulcata*. http://www.anapsid.org;sulcata.html.